How to S Monetizable YouTube Channel

How to Make Videos, Upload Them, Get Subscribers, and Start Making Money!

Maureen Oliver

Table of Contents

Part 1: *Creating Your YouTube Channel*

Chapter 1: *Choose a unique, easily searchable name for your YouTube channel*

Chapter 2: *Create a Gmail account, using your chosen channel name as your username*

Chapter 3: *You have studied YouTube's policies on Reused Content*

Chapter 4: *You have studied YouTube's policies on Spam, deceptive practices, & scams policies*

Chapter 5: *Your first video is ready to be uploaded*

Chapter 6: *Your YouTube channel art is ready and tested*

Part 2: *Before You Create Your First YouTube Video, Do This*

Part 3: *Before You Create A Youtube Ad, Read This!*

Chapter 1: *The First Thing You Need To Do BEFORE You Create A Youtube Ad*

Chapter 2: *What Type of YouTube Ad You Should Create*

Chapter 3: *The Best Way to Promote Your YouTube Video*

Chapter 4: *Another Way to Promote Your YouTube Video*

Part 4: *Secret Method You to Get Subscribers Fast!*

Part 5: *Final Notes*

All rights reserved. No part of this publication may be reproduced, distributed, or transmitted in any form or by any means, including photocopying, recording, or other electronic or mechanical methods, without the prior written permission of the publisher, except in the case of brief quotations embodied in critical reviews and certain other noncommercial uses permitted by copyright law.

Copyright © Maureen Oliver, 2002.

Part 1: *Creating Your YouTube Channel*

Chapter 1: *Choose a unique, easily searchable name for your YouTube channel*

If you have a good idea of what your channel is going to be about, then include it in your channel name. But don't let your channel name be too long.

Remember, people will have to type it into the YouTube search box each time they look for you. No one likes to have to type in a very long name.

How long should your channel name be?

I don't think it should be longer than five syllables. When choosing a channel name, ask yourself how you would like it if YOU had to type it into YouTube's search bar.

Consider those who have to look you up, by keeping your channel name short and sweet. So let's say your channel is about ASMR. You can simply call your channel Gabi ASMR, for instance.

Gabi being your name or nickname while ASMR tells us at once what your channel is about. If you are NOT worried about keeping your privacy, you can simply name your channel after yourself.

It is expected that BEFORE a person creates a YouTube channel, he knows what his channel is going to be about.

That's not fair. For you to comment on another YouTube video, you just have to have a channel - whether you like it or not!

And there it will lie, waiting for you to do something like some silent register of one's failures as the years go by and it still lies unused. Bah! Humburg!

Something should be done about that. That's if you're interested in making money from it.

But what if you don't know yet what your channel is going to be about and you just want it to develop as you go? Then you can just call it Gabi, for instance. But make sure Gabi hasn't been taken up by someone else.

To find out if your channel name is unique, just do a YouTube search of the name. Make sure you set the filters to Channels only.

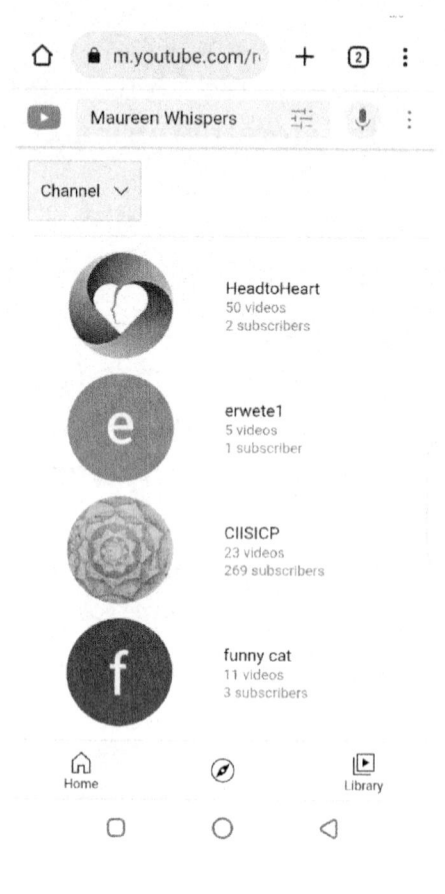

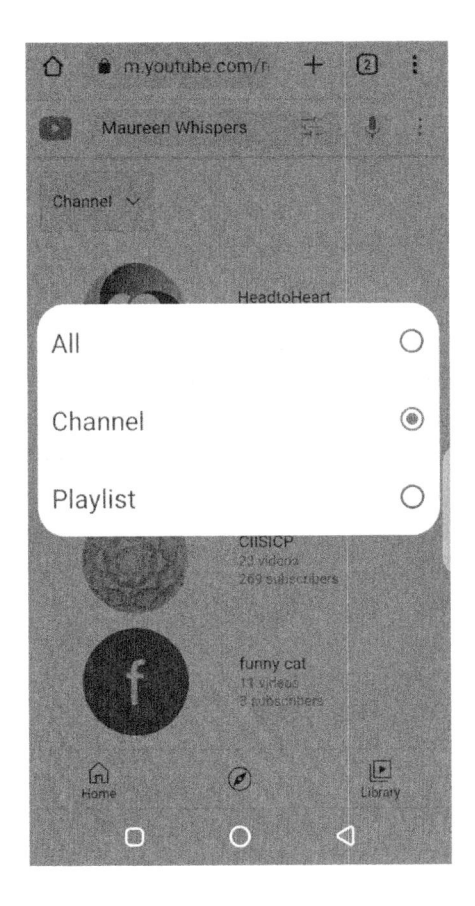

That's how I came up with the channel name, Maureen Whispers.

Don't create your channel yet!

And yes, I'm using a Smartphone - Android to be precise. So, we're talking about things

9

you do *BEFORE* you create a YouTube channel.

Chapter 2: *Create a Gmail account, using your chosen channel name as your username*

Running a YouTube channel is a business so choosing an email address that tallies with your YouTube channel name keeps things professional. You might want to share that email address with prospective sponsors or donors and also your viewers.

You may have to settle for a different version of your YouTube channel name, though. Yeah, MaureenWhispers@gmail.com was taken.

So you've chosen a name for your YouTube channel and created a Gmail account to create that channel. What else?

Do not create a YouTube channel until:

Chapter 3: *You have studied YouTube's policies on Reused Content*

If your ambition is to someday join the YouTube Partner Program, these two words are very important - *Reused Content*.

What is Reused Content?

Reused content refers to stuff you upload, that you did not create yourself, without adding *significant original commentary or educational value*.

So you just downloaded something then you uploaded it.

So many channels have failed to qualify for the YouTube Partner Program because of this, so be careful. Joining the YouTube Partner Program is the major way creators make money on YouTube.

The basic qualifications for joining the YouTube Partner Program are having:

- 1000 subscribers
- 4000 video watch hours within a year
- no community guideline strikes
- two-factor authentication enabled on your Google Account.

Also, avoid text-to-speech. Text-to-speech is regarded as templated or programmatically-generated repetitious content.

Repetitious content means videos on your channel are so similar, that people may have trouble spotting the difference between them.

YouTube likes variety and uniqueness. The surest way to make your videos unique is to add your real voice and/or face.

Do not create a YouTube channel until:

Chapter 4: *You have studied YouTube's policies on Spam, deceptive practices, & scams policies*

I lost three or four YouTube channels because of this.

For instance, you ask people for money in your videos, either verbally or in writing. Or you lead viewers away from YouTube to questionable sites.

They may not even have to be questionable. Just be careful about that. Don't create negative reviews about YouTube's sponsors.

Everybody is a sponsor so long as they have ever advertised on YouTube. Everybody is a potential sponsor so be careful about that.

Best to avoid it altogether. You never can tell with YouTube. There's more. So check out the links at the end of this book for YouTube policies on all this.

Do not create a YouTube channel until:

Chapter 5: *Your first video is ready to be uploaded*

Create at least three videos before you create a YouTube channel. Yeah, it will tell you whether you're going to be consistent, ok? Consistent means you're uploading at least once a week.

Post a video to YouTube three or more times per week, if possible. This can quickly raise your channel in the YouTube algorithm.

Me? I can only cope with uploading once a week. Because some of us have day jobs and we need time to create our videos.

And in some parts of the world, money for internet access - particularly in less developed countries.

Anyway, it's a good idea to have a good number of videos waiting before you create your YouTube channel.

Chapter 6: *Your YouTube channel art is ready and tested*

It's easy to create YouTube channel art using Canva.com. That includes your YouTube profile picture and banner. The term *channel art* covers both of these because you may use the same image for both your banner and your profile photo.

But be sure that the essential details of your channel, as displayed on the banner, can be viewed across all devices.

That means doing your best to keep vital information as much to the center of the banner as possible, as small as legible so that they appear across all devices.

2560px by 1440px is the ideal size for a YouTube channel art image (banner). The central area of 1546px by 423px is the safe area that will display on all devices.

Upload an image of at least 1546 x 423 pixels size, when deciding on your banner image for mobile devices. As a safe area that will be visible on mobile screens, this banner size is best.

The image will be automatically scaled down as per the width of the mobile device after you upload it. An app like Photo and Picture Resizer can help you with dimensions.

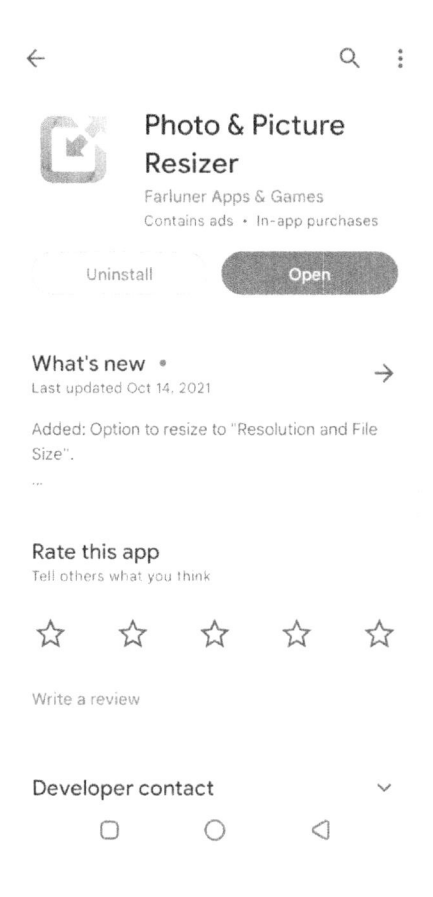

But if you don't want to bother your head about such things, just go straight to Canva.com and look for "YouTube banner."

22

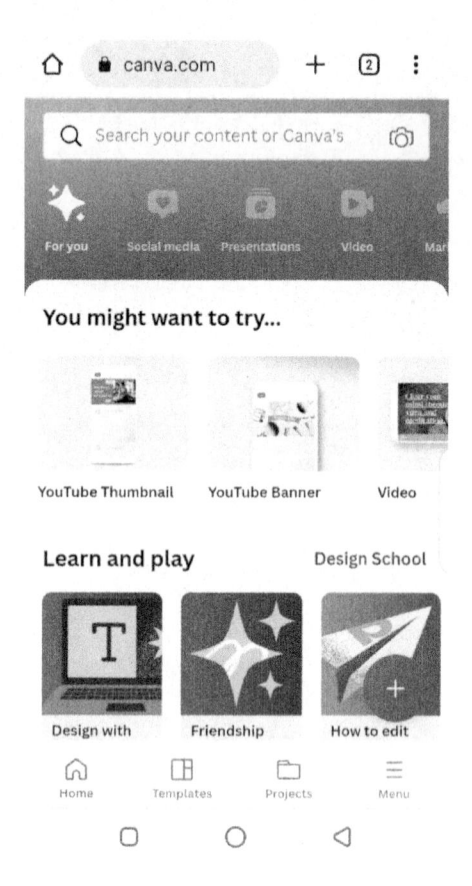

You can choose from a wide range of templates and with just a little editing, you're home-free.

When you finally decide to create your YouTube channel, first check out what your banner will look like on a mobile phone.

If it looks good on a phone, then it'll look good across all devices. You can easily do

24

that by trying to upload it via the YouTube app.

Yep, it means it's time to create your YouTube channel - making sure that your video(s) is/are ready to be uploaded.

You will see for yourself what your banner will look like beforehand, then you can make the necessary alterations if you are not satisfied with what you see.

You can see that my first attempt wasn't satisfactory since I couldn't get all the info to fit into that centermost bar.

So I went back to Canva.com and reduced the font size of the words. I also brought them all closer together. Funny how one doesn't follow one's instructions, huh?

See how they all now fit into that central space labeled "All devices"? Now let's see if the banner would also work as well, as a profile photo.

Yep. I think it would. Once you've created your YouTube channel, install Tubebuddy.

As you create your YouTube videos you will need Tubebuddy to guide you. It tells you all you need to do to make your videos more visible on YouTube.

Now I'm going to have to create a YouTube channel called Maureen Whispers before publishing this book. Wouldn't want it taken up by someone else after reading this book.

Hoping someone does read this book. Hey! I might create a YouTube series about my YouTube journey as Maureen Whispers.

Who knows? So why not keep an eye out for me?

YouTube Policies on Reused and Repetitious Content
https://support.google.com/youtube/answer/1311392?hl=en#zippy=%2Cfollow-adsense-program-policies

https://support.google.com/youtube/thread/123654864/channel-was-not-monetized-due-to-repetitive-content-videos-look-mass-produced-or-auto-generated?hl=en

YouTube Policies on Spam and Deceptive Practices
https://www.youtube.com/howyoutubeworks/policies/community-guidelines/

Part 2: *Before You Create Your First YouTube Video, Do This*

1. Install TubeBuddy

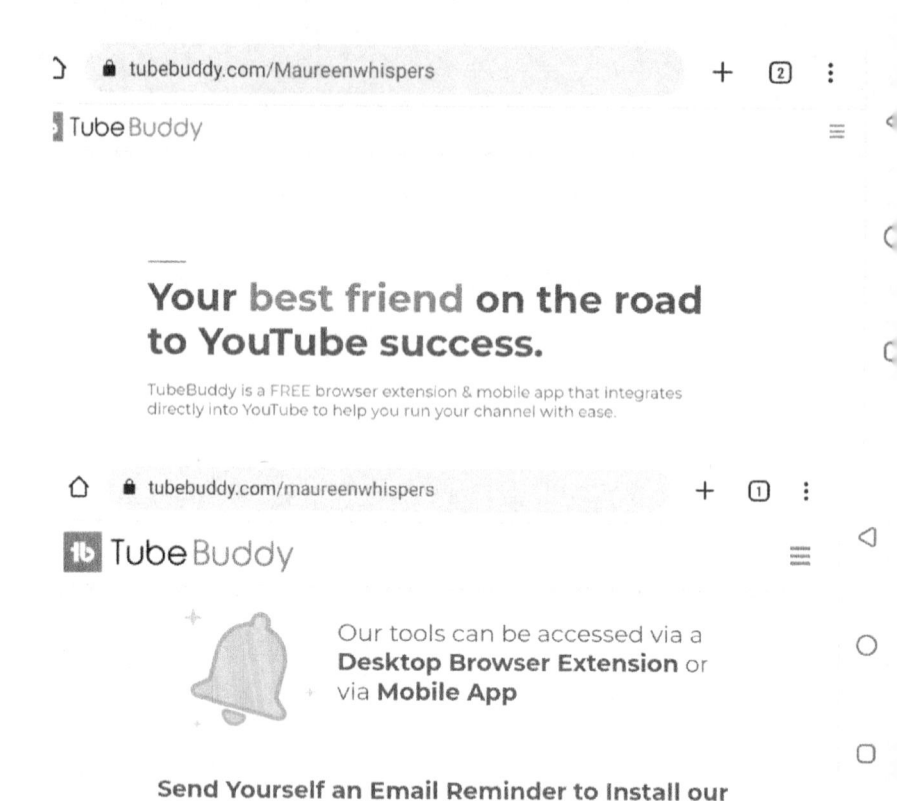

tubebuddy.com/Maureenwhispers

Tube Buddy

Your best friend on the road to YouTube success.

TubeBuddy is a FREE browser extension & mobile app that integrates directly into YouTube to help you run your channel with ease.

tubebuddy.com/maureenwhispers

Tube Buddy

Our tools can be accessed via a **Desktop Browser Extension** or via **Mobile App**

Send Yourself an Email Reminder to Install our Browser Extension

32

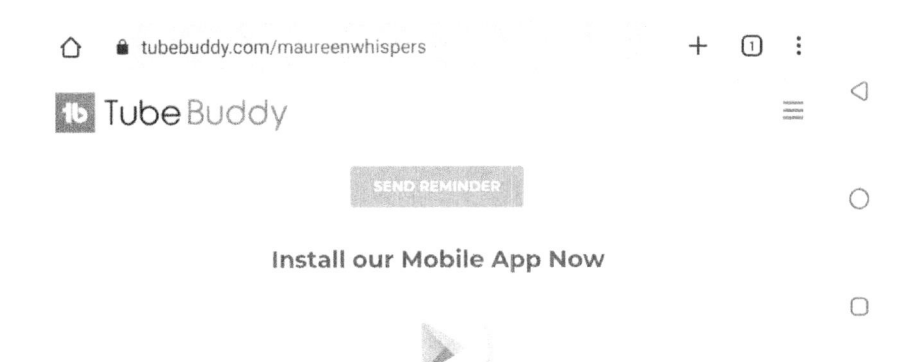

If you haven't created a YouTube channel yet, there's no point in installing TubeBuddy.

And yes, this book is targeted at Android phone users, although as you can see from the images above, TubeBuddy is available for both mobile and desktop users.

The same principles still generally apply to YouTubers, be they mobile or desktop users.

There are things you ought to do before you even consider creating a YouTube channel.

And no, they do NOT include buying expensive video equipment!

Before you create your first YouTube video:

2. Install CapCut

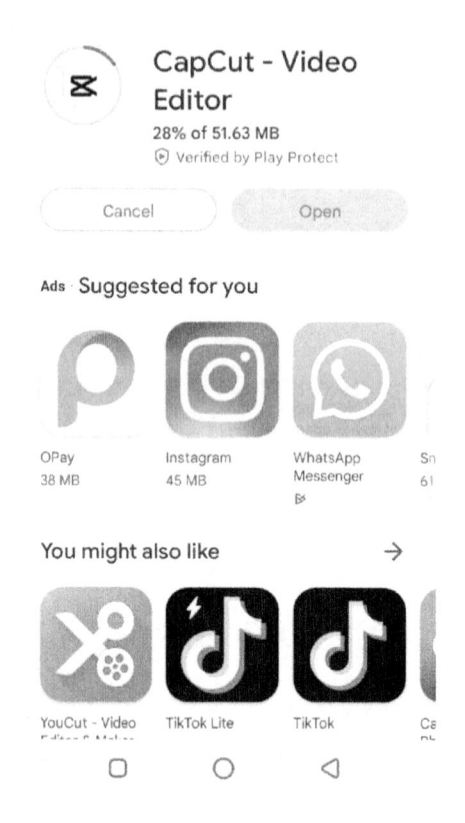

No, CapCut is not yet available for desktop devices – be it PC or laptops. It is only available for Android and iOS devices as a mobile app.

However, you can use an Android Emulator to install CapCut on your PC. After installing CapCut you may be tempted to create an intro for your YouTube videos.

DON'T.

Before you create your first YouTube video:

3. Forget about Creating a Channel Intro.

Create a hook instead, something to make the viewer want to keep watching your video. Like holding out a particular secret till the end of the video.

But telling them throughout the video that they have to keep watching if they want to know what that secret is.

People generally have short attention spans and if you can't hold their attention within the first eight to ten seconds of the video, they are likely not going to watch the rest of it.

Being able to retain the attention of your viewers matters, if you want YouTube to keep recommending your videos to viewers. Getting those recommendations is vital to the survival of your video.

Before you create your first YouTube video:

4. Create a YouTube Video Title

To create a hook, create a youtube video title first. E.g. Before You Create Your First YouTube Video, Do This! That's an idea, right?

Seriously, though. How do you come up with a title for your first video? If you already know what your channel is going to be about, then coming up with an idea for your first video shouldn't be hard.

Just do a video about it. But if you are still trying to figure out what your channel is going to be about, then you can begin by creating videos detailing your Youtube journey.

So let's say the title of your first YouTube video is Before You Create Your First YouTube Video, Do This! This is where TubeBuddy comes in.

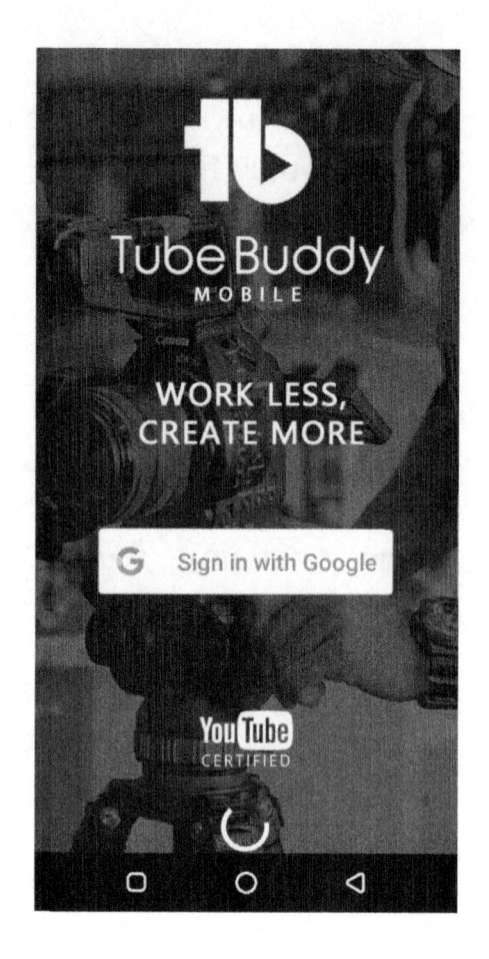

Sign in using the Gmail account you used to create your YouTube channel.

What we want to do is use TubeBuddy's Tag Explorer to see if we could get a better title for our video. We are looking for a title with a high search volume but relatively low competition.

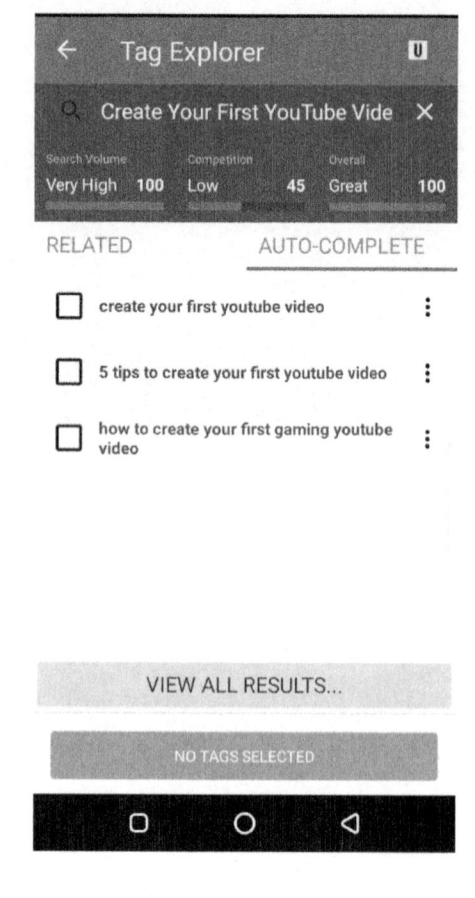

Turns out Create Your First YouTube Video is the best title for our first YouTube video, with a 100% score.

Before you create your first YouTube video:

5. Create A Script for Your Video

It's time to write down what you are going to say to viewers. It's as easy as opening a notepad and tapping the microphone icon on your Google keyboard.

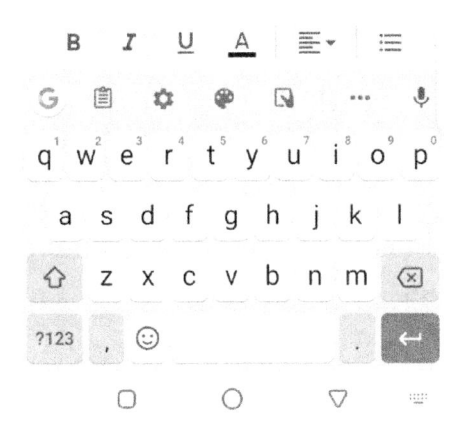

Begin to speak as soon as you are prompted by the keyboard to do so. Speak until you have nothing more to say on the subject matter. Then edit what you have said as taken down by the keyboard.

Keep editing till you are satisfied with the script. That's what you are going to tell your viewers in your video.

Before you create your first YouTube video:

6. Determine Your Target audience: Smartphone or PC Users?

This is important 'cause next you're going to use CapCut. You will need to decide how you want your video to be displayed.

9:16 is recommended if your target audience are smartphone users.

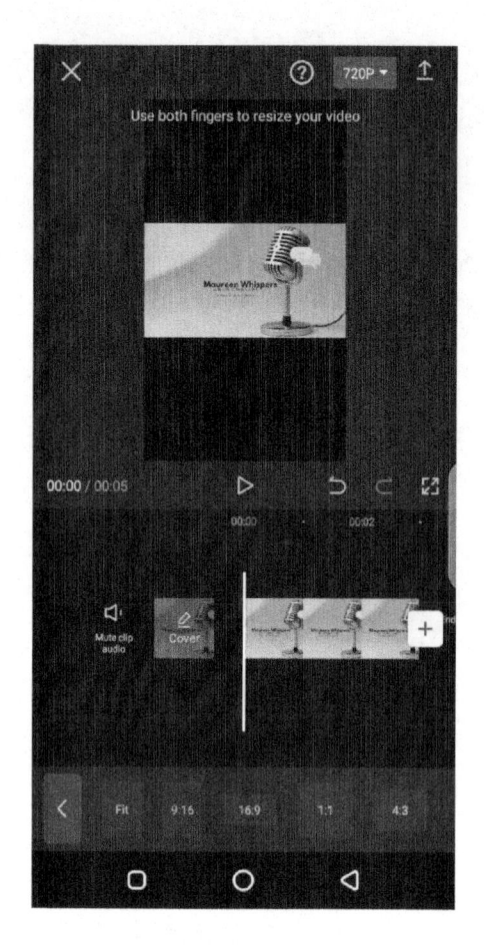

16:9 is recommended if your target audience are PC Users. If you are targeting both, then it's best to use 16:9.

Looks better anyway, doesn't it?

Like I said, keep the intro short, if you are going to use it all. Other than welcoming viewers to your channel, come to the point as soon as possible.

This particular image needs editing. The link in the image is against **YouTube's Spam, Scam & Deceptive Practices policies.**

https://bit.ly/3vGCdeh

To rectify this anomaly, we simply return to Canva.com and edit our channel banner.

So we can now go ahead and use it in CapCut.

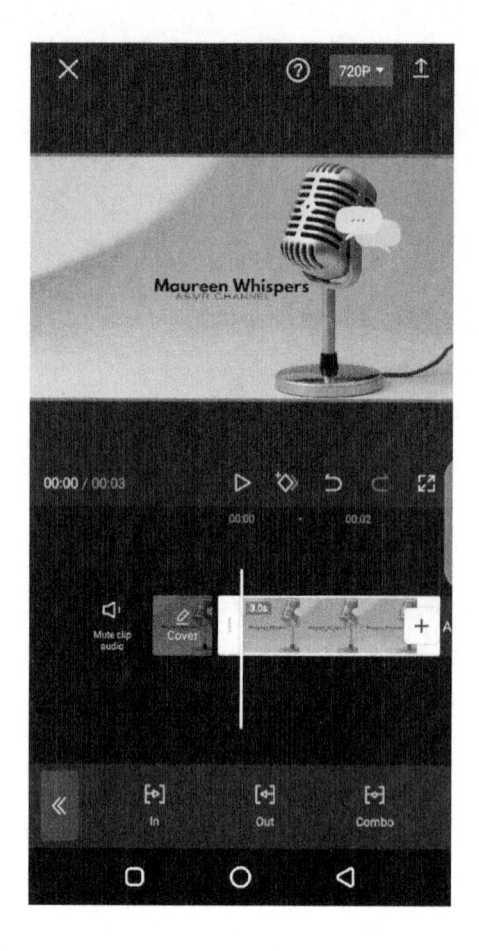

I set the image to Zoom in as the video progresses. You can see it doesn't last for more than three seconds. That should be long enough to say, "Hi. Welcome to Maureen Whispers!"

That's all the intro you need. I get tired of people who talk too much. I move on to the next video.

Next, go straight to the topic.

Before you create your first YouTube video:

7. Decide: Face or No Face?

Are you going to show your face or not in your videos?

Voice is mandatory.

Yeah, better to be on the safe side because YouTube is coming down pretty hard on unoriginal content these days.

Better to avoid using text-to-speech and stick to using your voice, if you want your channel monetized. This means if you want YouTube to someday start paying for the ads in your videos.

So, before you create your first YouTube video:

8. Avoid Reused and Repetitious Content, Text to Speech, AI-generated content, and Copyright Violations.

In other words, please study YouTube policies in general before you even create your YouTube channel. Best to study them, if you ever want YouTube to pay you money for uploading your videos.

https://bit.ly/2MwXKQy

If you are going to show your face, then go ahead and video yourself talking about the subject matter. Best to take several shots and merge them for variety.

YouTube is a jungle. It's no longer enough to just sit in front of a camera and talk continuously.

Vary it up.

If you decide you do not want to show your face, then create audio first. Create original video content to match your audio content. Edit and sync audio with video using CapCut.

I would advise you to avoid including subtitles, to avoid violating YouTube's policies on Reused and Repetitious Content.

https://bit.ly/3SqX8Mc

You also want to keep as much of the content as un-machine generated as possible to avoid trouble with YouTube when the time for monetization comes.

That's when you qualify to apply for the YouTube Partner Program. By then, you must have garnered 1,000 subscribers and 4000 watch hours within a year.

So, before you create your first YouTube video, you can read up on what it takes to qualify.

https://www.youtube.com/howyoutubeworks/policies/monetization-policies/

Somewhere in the video, include a CTA (Call-to-Action). For instance, Please Like, Comment, and Subscribe.

Probably best not to wait till the end of the video to say so because the viewer may stop watching before then.

Somewhere in the first few minutes of the video might be best. When you're done with your video, you can add an outro.

That too should be short. You may use it as another opportunity to include a final CTA. Go over your video to ensure you have made any mistakes.

To increase your earning potential, best to keep your videos at least 8 minutes long. You'll be able to insert an ad in the middle of the video when your channel finally gets monetized.

When you are satisfied with your entire video, click the Export arrow at the top.

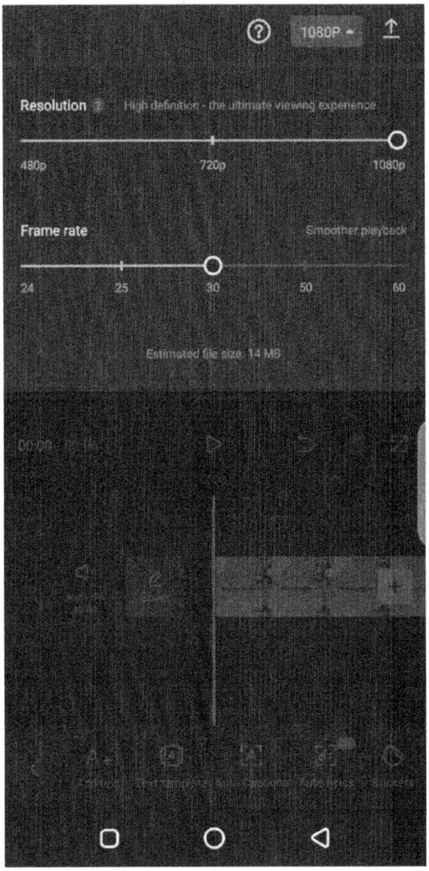
1080P
Resolution
High definition - the ultimate viewing experience
480p
720p
1080p
Frame rate
Smoother playback
24
25
30
50
60
Estimated file size: 14 MB

So you've created your first YouTube video. What's the title of your next video going to be? An idea for the next video will come to you from the script of the current one.

Part 3: *Before You Create A Youtube Ad, Read This!*

Chapter 1: *The First Thing You Need to do BEFORE You Create A YouTube Ad*

So you've created your first YouTube video and you want to promote it? Great!

In case you haven't created your first YouTube video yet, I think you should read my book BEFORE YOU CREATE YOUR FIRST YOUTUBE VIDEO, DO THIS - or don't even bother creating a Youtube video.

Then you can come back to this book. *It's important.* You may have missed something even if you already have a Youtube channel.

I said a lot in the book I'm not keen on repeating here. There's a lot more to uploading a Youtube video than *just* uploading a Youtube video - *if* you're interested in creating a Youtube channel that will get noticed.

Alright then, let's begin!

Chapter 2: *What Type of YouTube Ad You Should Create*

First off, how long does a video need to be to be able to promote it on YouTube ads? I created a very short video and was worried it was too short to promote via Youtube ads.

I should have known better. Have ever noticed these 5-second non-skippable video ads that pop up while you're watching a YouTube video?

There's my answer. If your video is less than 6 seconds, you can create a *Youtube bumper ad*. This way you are sure people will have to watch your ad - whether they like it or not!

That's the type I want but there are others.

Available video ad formats include:

- Skippable in-stream ads
- Non-skippable in-stream ads

- In-feed video ads
- Bumper ads
- Outstream ads
- Masthead ads

Let's *very* briefly talk about each one of them.

* *Skippable in-stream ads:* This one is self-explanatory. After 5 seconds, the viewer can skip the ad.

* *Non-skippable in-stream ads:* As the name implies, viewers don't have the option to skip the ad. But these video ads are up 15 seconds (or shorter).

Stay with me.

* *In-feed video ads:* I think a screenshot is in order here.

60

5:47 PM
YouTube
Explore
All
Live
Music
Nollyw
CODING
For Kids
Kids Age:6-16
BrightCHAMPS
WINDOW TO NEXTGEN SKILLS
BOOK NOW
Free Coding Classes for Kids
Ignite your child's growth by enabling them to explore their potential with BrightChamps.
Ad
BrightChamps
Home
Shorts
Subscriptions
Library

So you're scrolling up or down up or down Youtube and you see stuff like that - they're called in-feed video ads. That's how they look. So I'm done with that.

* *Outstream ads:* This should be good. Outstream ads aren't available on YouTube. (Well, thank goodness for that!) Outstream ads are mobile-only ads and only appear on websites and apps running on Google video partners.

* *Masthead ads*: They are only available on a reservation basis through a Google sales representative. Frankly, that's all I want to know.

For more detailed information about types of Youtube ads, visit Youtube Help.

Let's finally get on to the business of actually creating a YouTube ad!

Chapter 3: *One Way to Promote Your YouTube Video*

Once you're done reading, implementing everything you see in my book, uploaded your YouTube video, *AND COPIED THE LINK TO YOUR VIDEO,* go to YouTube Ads.

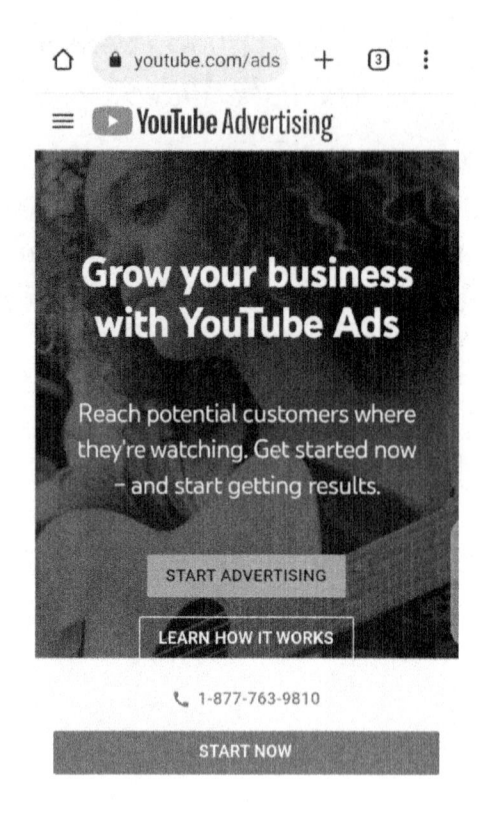

Click on *START NOW* - unless you have time to burn. Then you can click on *Learn How It Works.* Always a good idea though, but we're in a hurry!

On clicking *START NOW*, you will be directed to this page:

That's right. Create a Google Ads account if you don't already have one. Bookmark the page on your browser. It's important.

Now, let's see what happens when I click *NEW GOOGLE* ADS *ACCOUNT*.

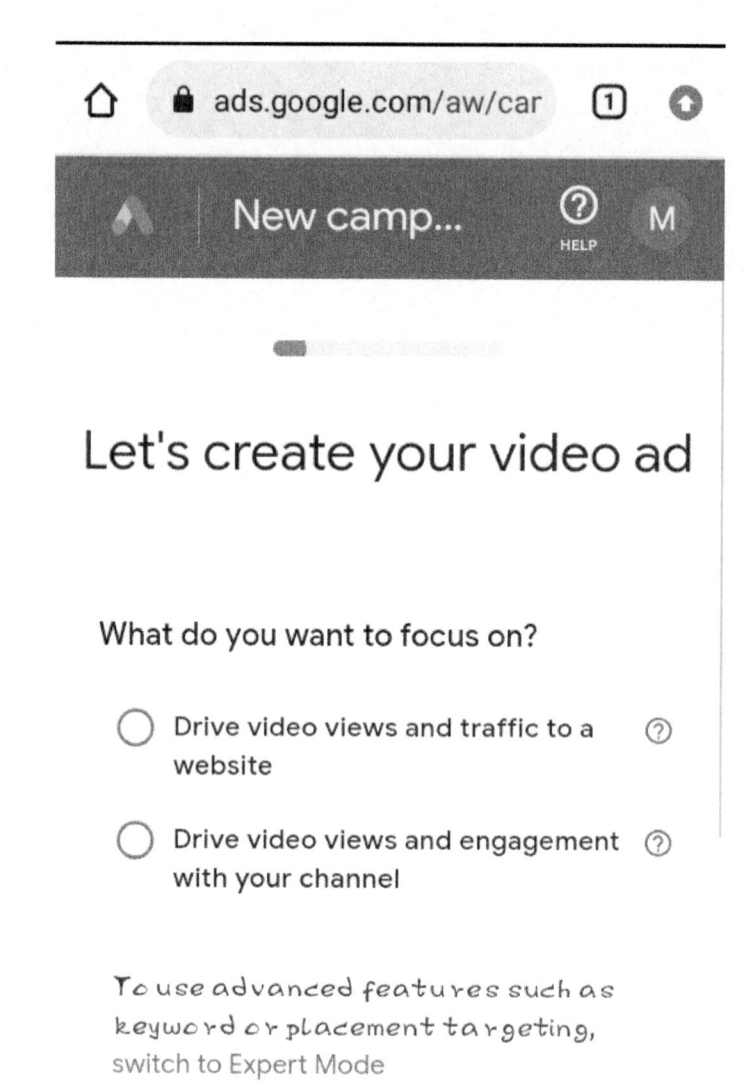

> ### Let's create your video ad
>
> **What do you want to focus on?**
>
> ○ Drive video views and traffic to a website
>
> ○ Drive video views and engagement with your channel
>
> *To use advanced features such as keyword or placement targeting,* switch to Expert Mode

Hooray! So let's choose *Drive video views and engagement with your channel* since

66

this is about promoting a YouTube channel, not a website. You can choose the latter option if it applies to you.

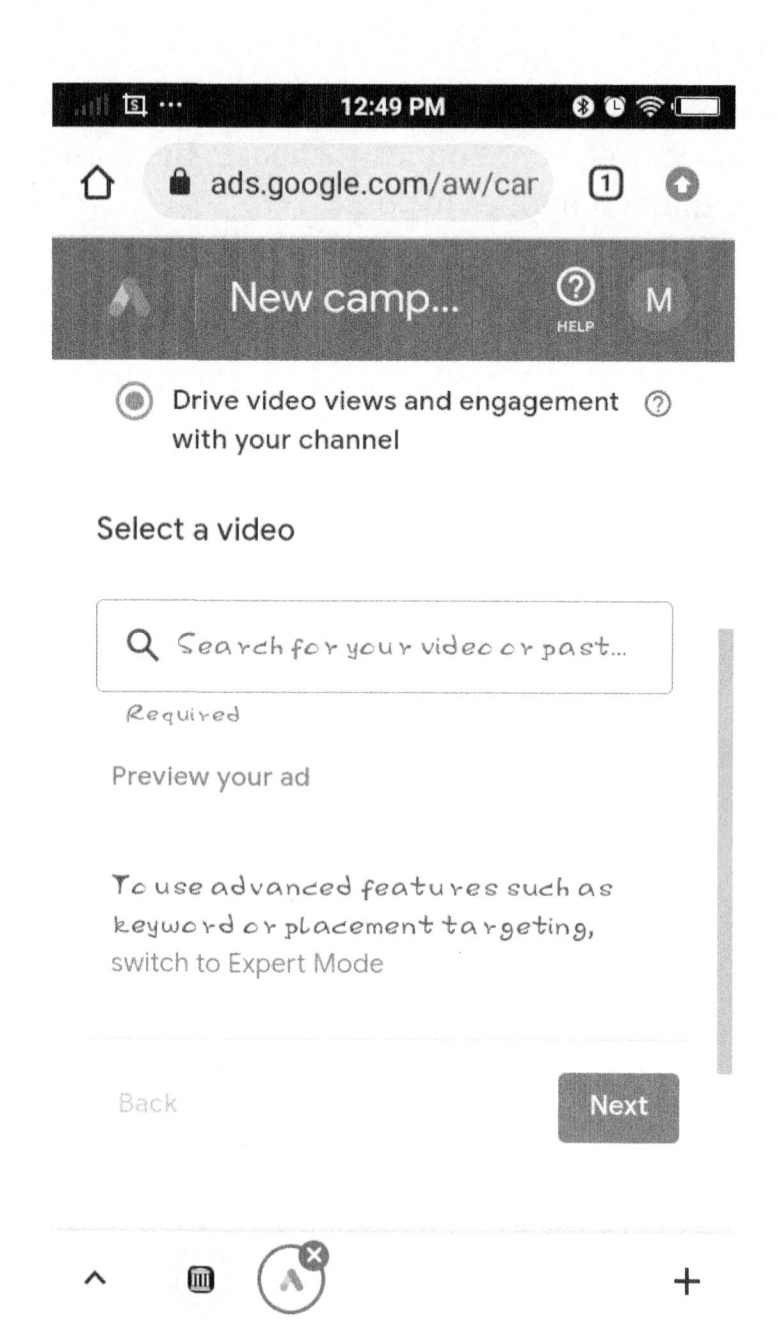

◉ Drive video views and engagement ⓘ
with your channel

Select a video

🔍 *Search for your video or past...*

Required

Preview your ad

To use advanced features such as keyword or placement targeting, switch to Expert Mode

Back   Next

Here, you get to search for your video. See? Easy!

⌂ 🔒 ads.google.com/aw/car ☐1 ⬆

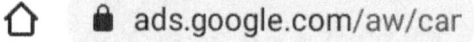

✕ | Maureen Whispers Loading...|

Jade – Paradise – Official 1900
by SadeVEVO • 25,718,032 views
Sade - Paradise Director - Alex]
03:37

Funeral Service for Maureen Orr
by CSG Funeral Home • 244 views
01:43:30

Proud Irish Traveller Sharyn Ward
by Ireland's Got Talent • 5,531,000 v
Proud Irish Traveller Sharyn Wa
08:15

Speeding Is The Answer To The Tr
by Dry Bar Comedy • 442,911 views
Speeding is the answer to the tra
07:51

As you can see, I can't find the video I'm looking for. Hence, the importance of copying the link to the video. After pasting the link instead into the box, this happens:

🏠 🔒 ads.google.com/aw/car 1️⃣ ⬆️

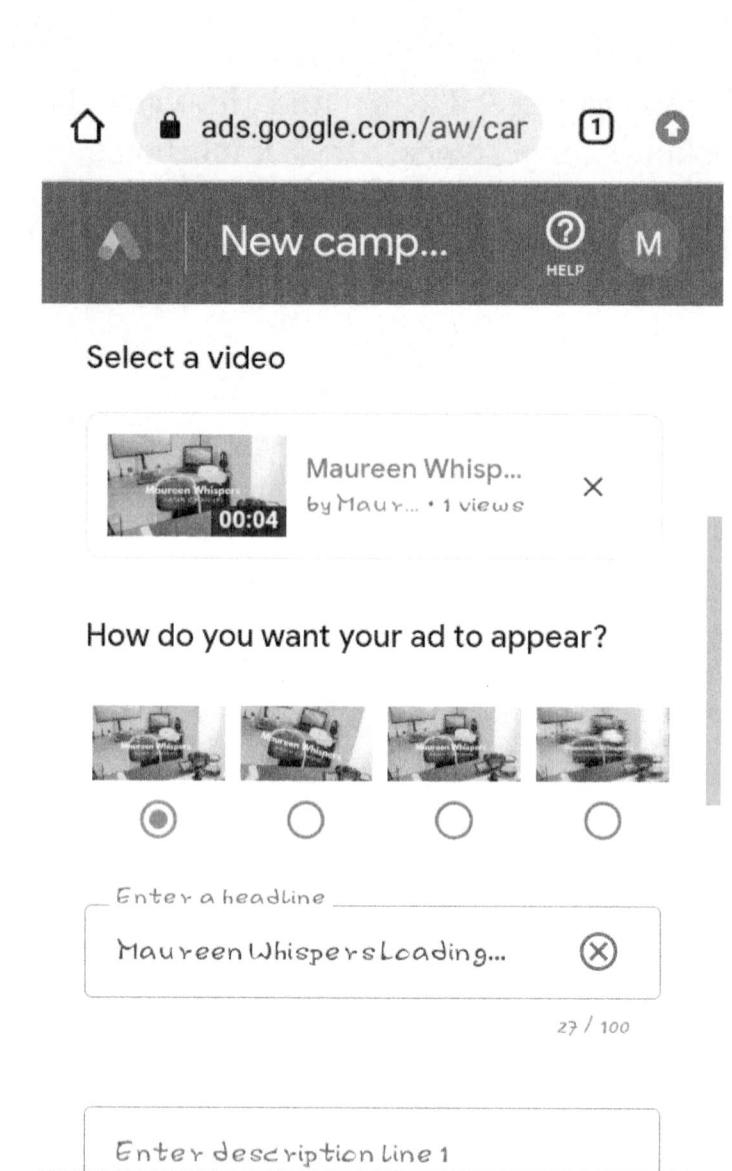

▲ New camp... ❓ M
               HELP

Select a video

[video thumbnail 00:04] Maureen Whisp... ✕
by Mau r... • 1 views

How do you want your ad to appear?

(●) ( ) ( ) ( )

Enter a headline
┌─────────────────────────────┐
│ Maureen WhispersLoading... ⊗│
└─────────────────────────────┘
                      27 / 100

┌─────────────────────────────┐
│ Enter description line 1   │

72

The video I want comes up. I decided to trim my video to 4 seconds, just to be on the safe side. Sometimes you'll create a video to a certain length of time, only for you to upload it and discover it's gotten longer on YouTube.

It's happened to me several times so if Youtube says less than 6 seconds, it's best to keep it to 4 seconds when you're editing the video!

Next:

How do you want your ad to appear
Enter a headline
Enter a description, etc.

All this stuff is easy. So more screenshots, less talk!

🏠 🔒 ads.google.com/aw/car ① ⬆

New camp... ? HELP M

Your video

Maureen Whisper...
by Mauree... • 1 views

How your ad shows

Placed as a thumbnail next to related videos or on the YouTube homepage   ✏️

Headline

Maureen Whispers Loading...

Description

ASMR Channel Launch
Expect Only Whispers

Estimated impressions	Estimated views
6.3K - 14K per week	150 - 310 per week

74

Chapter 4: *Another Way to Promote Your YouTube Video*

Log in to studio.youtube.com

Click on the Play button you see on the left-hand panel. It will take you to your youtube video uploads.

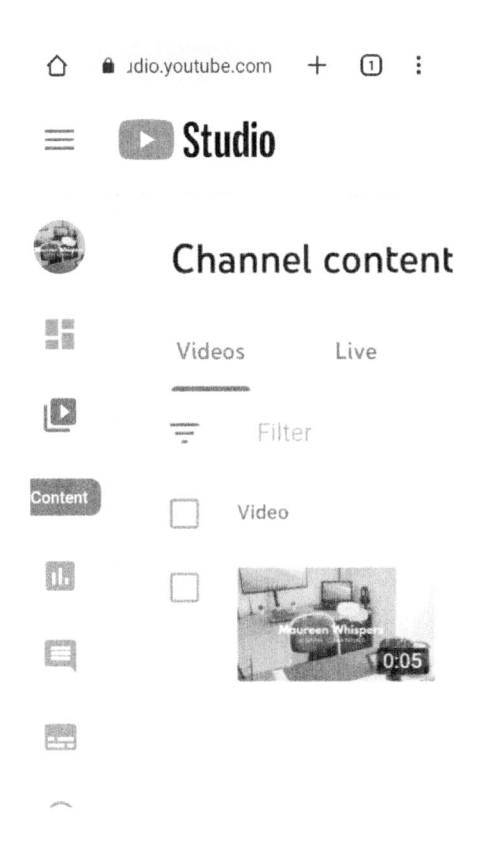

Yes, I use a smartphone, an Android phone to be precise, but the same principles apply to both mobile and PC users.

Now, tap to the right of the particular video you want to promote, but **NOT** on the name of the video itself. If you do the latter, it will lead you to edit the video details. That's not where we're going here.

Tap to the side of the thumbnail for the video.

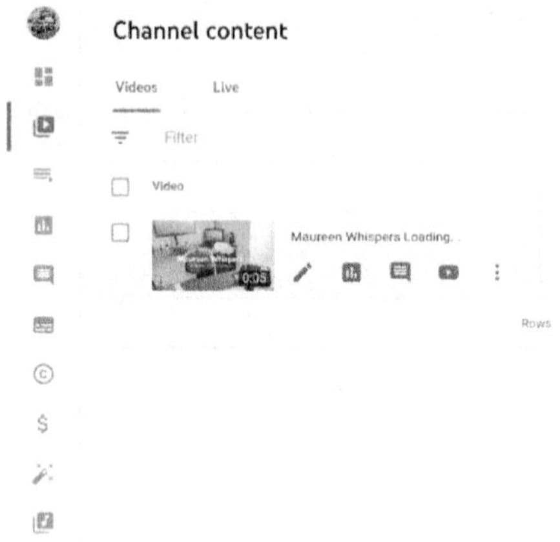

Next, tap on those three dots at the side of the icons that pop up. A list of options will come up and one of them is ***Promote.*** That's what we want. Click on Promote.

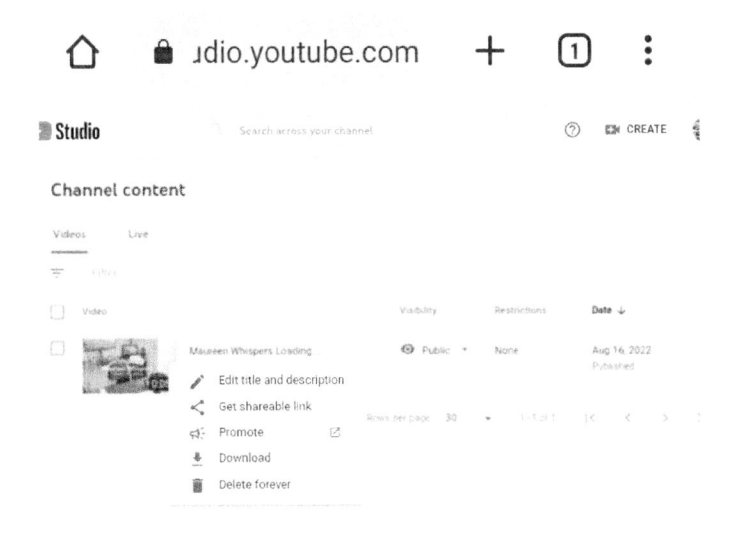

When you click on *Promote*, you will be taken to this page:

You know what to do next.

Part 4: *How To Get Subscribers Fast!*

Chapter 1: *Secret Method You Can Use to Get Subscribers Fast!*

If you want Subscribers to come to your channel naturally and quickly, then you have to upload videos *at least once a day.*

If you are uploading *quality, informative,* and/or *entertaining* content *every day,* that you created yourself, at least once a day for a month and your Subscriber count is not increasing, then you can go ahead and delete your YouTube channel because you have nothing to offer.

If you have determined NOT to delete your YouTube channel, then there are some things you can do, as I have said earlier.

It's also a good idea to ask people, in your videos, in your description, and in your comments section, to Subscribe.

Some include a *DO NOT CLICK* shortened link to their Youtube channel that will ask you whether you want to Subscribe or not.

Here's the format:

https://www.youtube.com/channel/<YOUR CHANNEL ID>?sub_confirmation=1

For example:

https://www.youtube.com/channel/UCG57sNeLTEw25Yz9utyPuDA?sub_confirmation=1

The shortened version will look like this:

https://bit.ly/3KkQmUr

Your channel URL will look something like this to start with:

https://m.youtube.com/channel/UCG57sNeLTEw25Yz9utyPuDA

That part of the link after "channel/" is YOUR CHANNEL ID.

When you click the shortened link (the bit.ly link above) you'll see something like:

youtube.com/channel/UCG57sNeLTEw25Yz9utyPuDA
Maureen Whispers
Confirm channel subscription
Are you sure you want to subscribe to Maureen Whispers?
CANCEL
SUBSCRIBE

Unfortunately, that dialogue box only shows up in the desktop version. In the mobile version, the link takes the visitor directly to your channel page, which really isn't a bad thing.

Either way, the visitor has the option of deciding to Subscribe or not.

Finally, we come to a *secret method you can use to get Subscribers fast.*

Now for the secret method for getting Subscribers fast.

Upload very popular videos.

The kind that people love to watch or even listen to, even though you know it won't get approved for the Youtube Partner Program.

At least once a day is best for optimum results although you will have to *delete them once you hit 2,000 Subscribers* - not 1000. It has to be at least 2000 Subscribers because, by the time you start uploading stuff that will get your channel approved, people may start unsubscribing. After all, that's not what they signed up for. The extra 1,000 is to make allowances for the drop in Subscriber count.

Examples of very popular videos include music videos, collections of songs by popular artists, movie trailers, old movies, meditation videos, radio dramas, and audiobooks.

I didn't include TikTok compilation videos because it is possible to get those approved by simply adding extensive voice commentaries to them.

You can now go ahead and upload your *real* videos. To check how many watch hours they have accumulated, check each of them in Youtube Studio. When you have accumulated the required 4000 watch hours, you can go over to your Monetization page in Youtube Studio to apply to join the Youtube Partner Program.

Yeah, if you check Maureen Whispers it's currently at 15 subscribers, at the time of writing this book because I am tired of YouTube's BS and I am simply keeping that channel for tutorial purposes. You know, like when you have to explain stuff to people in a book!

15 subscribers! That's about $6 worth of Youtube ads. Costly if you ask me. The really funny part is that I only got charged for those 15 Subscribers *AFTER* I'd gone to a *Youtube views exchange* site and got about 40 Subscribers on my own from there.

86

Youtube of course scrapped all of them, except for 15, so I'm not even sure Youtube was responsible for those 15.

All I know is I got charged for them, immediately after I had gone to that site, though for days *AFTER* putting up the Youtube ad, I had zero Subscribers.

It would be interesting to know if another visit to that site would get me charged again by Youtube ads. The whole thing smells fishy to me.

What happened was that Youtube dropped the number of Subscribers to 2!

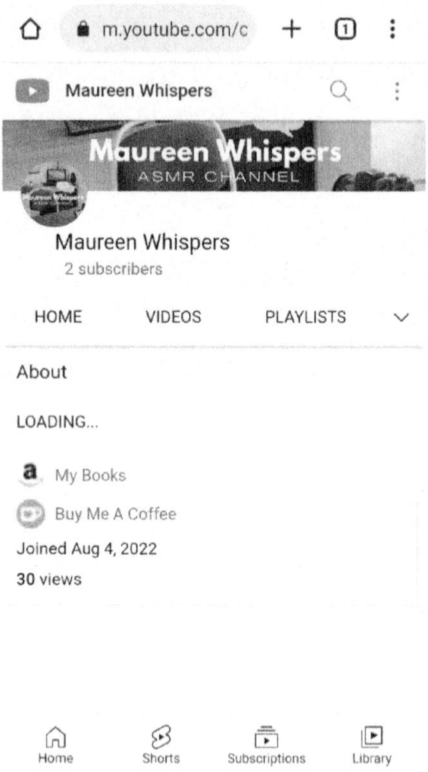
m.youtube.com/c
Maureen Whispers
Maureen Whispers
ASMR CHANNEL
Maureen Whispers
2 subscribers
HOME
VIDEOS
PLAYLISTS
About
LOADING...
My Books
Buy Me A Coffee
Joined Aug 4, 2022
30 views
Home
Shorts
Subscriptions
Library

Wow! As you can see Youtube won't allow you to cheat the system to get more subscribers.

Wish they didn't have to charge me $8 to prove a point though. So I essentially paid $8 for 2 Subscribers. One of them is from another account. So I paid $8 to get 1 Subscriber.

Done with Youtube ads!

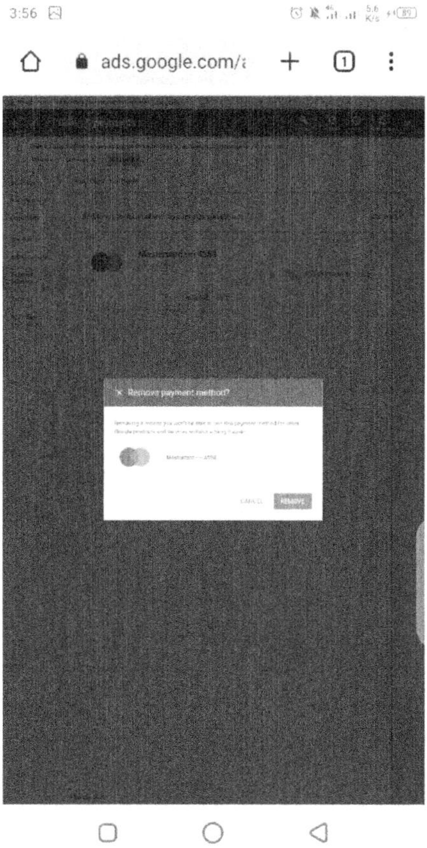
3:56
ads.google.com/a
Remove payment method?

Thank goodness that's over. So we're left with the *secret formula!*

I wrote a book called *Ten Reasons Why You Should Delete Your Youtube Channel Right Now!* If you think being a successful

92

Youtuber is going to be easy, I think you should read it.

YouTube can decide to ban your channel at any time no matter what you tell them - and they don't even need to give you a tangible excuse for doing so.

I can say this with confidence because it's happened to me quite several times which is why I'm not too keen on growing a new one.

Oh well!

Part 5: Final Notes

1. Be prepared to work your ass off!

If you want to be a successful, professional YouTuber, you *must* invest time.

If you have a day job, you Youtube at night - and hope for some sleep before you have to go to work again. If you're lucky, you may get 4 hours of sleep. That's how dedicated you have to be if you want to succeed on YouTube.

Because you need to make out time to do research, create your script, create your video, edit your video, upload your video, and promote your video.

(God! Am I going to have to go through all that again?)

2. Youtube *may turn down your* application

You decided to create a YouTube channel. You uploaded all this great content (at least you thought so), only for you to apply for monetization, and guess what?

YouTube turns you down. All those months of hard work down the drain, 'cause once YouTube turns you down, it's unlikely they'll accept you until you make some *extensive* changes to your content.

Yeah, you should probably study ALL their *monetization policies* before you even consider starting a YouTube channel to earn money.

Just remember that you need at least 1000 Subscribers and 4000 watch hours before you can apply to join the YouTube Partner Program.

Honestly, YouTube has so many policies in place, that the surest way to ensure you

95

don't fall foul of any of them is to *just sit in front of a camera and talk sense,* being sure to merge several takes rather than just produce a long continuous unvarying video.

3. If your phone sucks, get a better one

If you have a low-memory phone like mine, creating and uploading quality videos on YouTube is going to be a challenge.

You want to create original videos so you don't fall foul of YouTube's Reused Content policy.

If your phone sucks, you're going to need a lot of light, like daylight. So I'd suggest taking most of your shots outside in bright daylight, even if you don't want to show your face.

If videoing is not your thing, and you're just thinking of editing stuff and putting them together, you're taking a risk. Youtube is pretty tough these days, so watch out. *Keyword: Reused Content.*

4. Being a YouTuber is costly

The average price of 1GB of data in my part of the world is $2.78

I thought that was expensive until I checked and discovered that the US on average charges $12.37 for 1GB of data, making it the 4th most expensive in the world!

My God! How do they do it? Yet the most successful YouTubers in the world are Americans. That's the American spirit for you.

I will never complain about the cost of data in my country again! Yeah well, I still think most Americans earn more than people from other countries so they can probably afford to pay that much.

Anyway, data costs money, any way you look at it. And if you are not prepared to invest not just time but money as well, to see that your channel succeeds, then forget about making money from it.

Eventually, you'll probably be spending a lot more than data. That's what it takes to be Number 1.

5. One day, you may just be plain tired of YouTube like me

If each time you create a YouTube channel, it gets banned, eventually, you're bound to get tired even when you know it's your fault.

There are certain types of videos that get you, subscribers, quickly - yes. Unfortunately, this usually involves uploading copyrighted content. The only way you can make money from such channels is *to ask for donations or share affiliate programs,* either one of which may still get you in trouble with Youtube for *Spam, Scams, and Deceptive Practices*. Eventually, if uploading copyrighted content gets you 3 copyright strikes - and you're out.

So either you do it the hard way and upload content that belongs to you so you don't lose your channel. Or you keep trying to do things the easy way by uploading stuff that doesn't belong to you - and *maybe* lose your channel.

Me, I'm sort of in the tired stage. I'm not much of an inspiration, I know, but you need to know what you're getting into trying to create a YouTube channel that will make you money.

It's serious business. So don't f*** around.

6. Watch out for creepy stalkers

Yes, it does happen. Watch this video. It's about this creepy stalker on YouTube called

Jack the Ripper. Not the real one but this one was creepy enough. The video is by this channel called TheTekkitRealm.

And I'm done.

Thanks for stopping by.

Bye!

Love,
Maureen

Printed in Great Britain
by Amazon